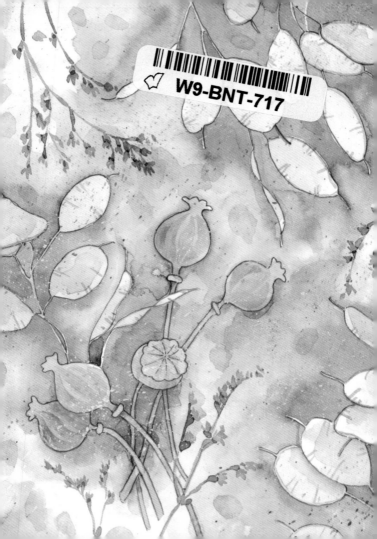

Other giftbooks by Helen Exley

...And Wisdom Comes Quietly
A Special Gift of Wisdom
Thank You For Your Kindness
To a very special Friend
Words on Calm
To someone special Wishing You Happiness

Published simultaneously in 2002 by Exley Publications Ltd
in Great Britain, and Exley Publications LLC in the USA.

2 4 6 8 10 12 11 9 7 5 3

ISBN 1-86187-423-5

A copy of the CIP data is available from the British Library on request.

Created and selected by Helen Exley.
Illustrated by Juliette Clarke.
Printed in China.

Exley Publications Ltd
16 Chalk Hill, Watford, Herts, WD19 4BG, UK

Exley Publications LLC,
185 Main Street, Spencer, MA 01562, USA

www.helenexleygiftbooks.com

A SPECIAL GIFT
MY WISHES
FOR YOU

Illustrated by Juliette Clarke
A HELEN EXLEY GIFTBOOK

FOR YOU... A LIFE OF JOY!

*My wish for you, is that life's party
is always filled with joy and laughter.*

STUART AND LINDA MACFARLANE

*May your life be like a wild flower,
growing freely in the beauty
and joy of each day.*

NATIVE AMERICAN

*May you have warm words
on a cold evening,
a full moon on a dark night,
and a smooth road all the way
to your door.*

IRISH TOAST

May you always choose
the right fork in the road.

–

Wherever you go, we your family and friends
are here for you – as you are for us.

PETER GRAY, B.1928

Good Luck!
Wherever you choose to go,
may the land you're in be without tragedy.
May the women, the children,
the men welcome you.
May you be surrounded by the beauty
of trees and flowers.
May you meet good and honest people.
May you be happy and at peace.

HELEN THOMSON, B.1943

MAY YOUR LIFE
HAVE DIAMOND DAYS.

PAM BROWN, B.1928

May the years to come bring you
all that you hope for – and glorious
astonishments you have never dreamed of!

PAM BROWN, B.1928

May the longtime sun shine upon you,
all love surround you,
and the sweet light within you
guide your way on.

AUTHOR UNKNOWN

May you live each second with joy.
May you live each minute with hope.
May you live each hour with patience.
May you live each day with wonder.
And may your year be filled with peace
and love.

STUART AND LINDA MACFARLANE

I HOPE YOU FIND JOY
IN THE GREAT THINGS
OF LIFE — BUT ALSO
IN THE LITTLE THINGS.
A FLOWER, A SONG,
A BUTTERFLY
ON YOUR HAND.

ELLEN LEVINE

*May you find
the little paths
bright with birdsong,
hedged with flowers.*

CHARLOTTE GRAY, B.1937

SMALL THINGS

*Never lose an opportunity of seeing anything
that is beautiful.... Welcome beauty in every
fair face, in every fair sky, in every flower....*

RALPH WALDO EMERSON
(1803-1882)

*I WISH YOU THE JOY OF SMALL PLEASURES –
– home-baked bread, fresh eggs, sun after rain,
– a smile in passing,
– the purple and gold at the heart
of a scarlet pimpernel,
– the swallow's rust-feathered throat,
– the delicate hands of a mouse,
– the jewel-like eyes of a toad,
– mist across meadows,
– lamp-shine on wet footpaths,
– rain-patter marching the streets.
Wonders are all about you.*

PAM BROWN, B.1928

I WISH YOU THE LUCK OF...

...finding a long-sought, long-out-of-print book in a garage sale.

...finding that the stain down the front of your new overcoat does, after all, come out.

...finding the last piece of the jigsaw.

...finding the silver propelling pencil that has been missing for a year down the back of the sofa, together with the nail scissors, half a packet of old licorice, a pile of coins, a pair of socks and a darning needle.

...opening the oven door and finding the soufflé has risen.

—

MAY YOU ALWAYS...

...get the front door open and charge
to the phone before it stops ringing.
...say the right thing to the wine waiter.
...have enough money to get home.
...remember your zipper.
...find exactly the right retort – succinct,
memorable, overwhelming – <u>at the time</u>
and not half an hour later.

–

MAY YOU NEVER...

...lose your keys, passport, wallet,
credit card, purse, tickets, hold-all,
spectacles, watch – or the bit of paper
with the vital phone number on it.

PAM BROWN, B.1928

IRISH TOASTS

May the road rise to meet you.
May the wind be always
at your back, the sun shine
warm upon your face,
the rain fall soft upon your
fields... and may God hold you
in the hollow of his hand.

—

Here's a health to thine and thee,
not forgetting mine and me.
When thine and thee again meet mine
and me, may mine and me have as much
welcome for thine and thee
as thine and thee have had for mine
and me today.

—

May the frost never afflict your spuds.
May the outside leaves of your cabbage
always be free from worms.
May the crows never pick your haystack,
and may your donkey always be in foal.

—

Health and long life to you.
The husband of your choice to you.
A child every year to you.
Land without rent to you.
And may you be half-an-hour in heaven
before the devil knows you're dead.
Sláinte! (Health!)

—

*...clear rivers
and
calm seas!*

FROM
"SHARE THE HOPE"

MAY YOU FIND PEACE

Deep peace, pure white of the moon to you;
Deep peace, pure green of the grass to you;
Deep peace, pure brown of the earth to you;
Deep peace, pure grey of the dew to you,
Deep peace, pure blue of the sky to you!
Deep peace of the running wave to you,
Deep peace of the flowing air to you,
Deep peace of the quiet earth to you.

FIONA MACLEOD

Leave home in the sunshine:
Dance through a meadow –
Or sit by a stream and just be.
The lilt of the water
Will gather your worries
And carry them down to the sea.

J. DONALD WALTERS

WISHING YOU DAYS
OF SUNSHINE AND JOY

Walk on a rainbow trail; walk on a trail of song,
and all about you will be beauty.
There is a way out of every dark mist,
over a rainbow trail.

NAVAJO SONG

*May we walk with grace and may the light
of the universe shine upon our path.*

AUTHOR UNKNOWN

MAY YOUR LIFE BE BLESSED WITH LONG SPRINGS
AND SHORT WINTERS.

HELEN THOMSON, B.1943

*May the blessing of light be on you,
light without and light within.
May the blessed sunshine
shine on you and warm your heart
till it glows like a great peat fire,
so that the stranger may come
and warm himself at it,
and also a friend.*

TRADITIONAL IRISH BLESSING

I WISH YOU THE WONDER
OF THE WORLD

May you find great treasure –
flowers and pebbles, sunlight and starlight,
birdsong and butterflies.
Marvels and mysteries.

I wish you the beauty of silence,
the glory of sunlight, the mystery of darkness,
the force of flame,
the power of water, the sweetness of air,
the quiet strength of earth, the love that lies
at the very root of things.

—

We are a part of all that is.
The branching trees find echoes in our veins.
The Spring that calls
the buds to break and the swallows
to return wakens us to joy.
May you, today and always,
share the wonder of the world.

PAM BROWN, B.1928

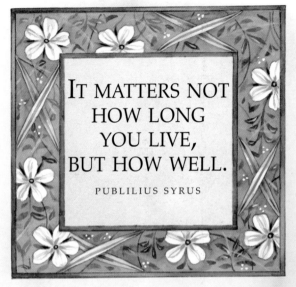

IT MATTERS NOT HOW LONG YOU LIVE, BUT HOW WELL.

PUBLILIUS SYRUS

May you never feel corrupted by empty wealth,
possessions or time-wasting pursuits.
But may you be able to love deeply, grow strong
friendships, have timely rewarding work and
develop that central base to
happiness, a commitment to your own
personal values.

HELEN EXLEY

I wish you the happiness of always having
something to give;
– a surprise, affection,
– freshly-baked scones, paperbacks,
seedlings and apples,
– a fetching-in of shopping,
a hand with the tidying up,
a feeding of cats,
a finding of plumbers
– a listening ear
– comfort
– time.

PAM BROWN, B.1928

Just on very rare and special moments
may something you do or say
make all the difference to someone's life.

MAYA V. PATEL, B.1943

I hope your personal dreams come true:

...that the men of the world choose
the path of peace.

...that you live to see the beauty of the next spring
and many more.

...that you work steadily at your vocation
and become outstandingly skilled.

...that all the world's children have clean water,
fresh air, whole natural food.

...that you grow to love one person madly,
blissfully, until the end of your life.

—

I hope that you have one piece of ridiculous
stupendous luck:

...like a mammoth lottery win.

...like a long meeting with the person
you most admire.

...like becoming a star, a leader.
...like taking a long, long holiday in a place
that captures your heart.

HELEN EXLEY

May you always know
the peace and joy of love.

STUART AND LINDA
MACFARLANE

TO LOVE!

Live every moment of your life in love!

STUART AND LINDA MACFARLANE

I WISH YOU THE JOY OF THE RIGHT ONE
REALIZING JUST WHO YOU REALLY ARE
INSIDE — AND LOVING YOU FOR IT.

PETER GRAY, B.1928

I wish you love. Romance, yes. But, too,
the love of those who lie together in the darkness,
talking of times past. The reassuring touch,
the lighting up of eyes, the sound of a key
in the lock.

CHARLOTTE GRAY, B.1937

To fall in love is only a beginning.
The true joy of love is only shaped by time.
I wish you that discovery, that happiness.

PAM BROWN, B.1928

I wish you the joy of tree-lined country lanes
and deep, lost greenway tracks, roads over
the high moors – harebells and hidden spring.
Roads bucketing down hillsides to the sea.

The road to Rome, the road to the sea.

The road to the Isles. The road home.

PAM BROWN, B.1928

BLESSINGS

Blessings of a kind heart upon you;
Blessings of the eyes of compassion upon you;
Blessings of giving to the earth upon you;
Blessings of the wisdom of the seasons upon you;
Blessings of breathing freely upon you;
Blessings of this moment upon you.

JACK KORNFIELD

May happiness come.
May corn come.
Just as the farmers work
And look forward to the reaping,
So may we sit again as we are
sitting now.

THE GA OF GHANA ON THE NEW YEAR FESTIVAL

TODAY, TODAY, TODAY. BLESS US...
AND HELP US TO GROW.

FROM THE ROSH HASHANAH LITURGY

May you be happy.
May you be peaceful.
May you be free from suffering.
As I want to be happy, peaceful, and free
from suffering, may you be happy, peaceful,
and free from suffering.

BUDDHIST METTA LOVING-KINDNESS PRAYER

May suffering ones be suffering free
And the fear-struck fearless be.
May the grieving shed all grief —
And the sick find health relief.

ZEN CHANT

MAY EVERYONE BE HAPPY
AND SAFE

As plentiful as the grass that grows,
Or the sand on the shore,
Or the dew on the lea,
So the blessings of the King of Grace
On every soul that was, that is, or will be.

TRADITIONAL IRISH BLESSING

May everyone be happy and safe,
and may their hearts be filled with joy.
May all living beings live in security
and in peace –
...May all of them dwell in perfect tranquility.
Let no one do harm to anyone.
Let no one put the life of anyone in danger.
Let no one, out of anger or ill will,
wish anyone any harm.

FROM METTA SUTTA (SUTTANIPATA),
TRANSLATED BY THICH NHAT HANH, B.1926

MAY YOU BUILD A LIFE
WORTH THE LIVING

May you never cease to search and challenge.
May you discover what you want to do
and do it well.

—

I wish you the happiness of mastering
a new skill, completing a task
to your own satisfaction, finding
you understand something that has till
now defeated you, discovering something
you never knew before.

—

May you meet the future with hope and courage,
enthusiasm, energy and joy. Take them
all and from them build a life that's
worth the living.

PAM BROWN, B.1928

A FRIEND!

A little health, a little wealth,
a little house
and freedom. And at the end,
a little friend, and little
cause to need him.

FROM
A NINETEENTH CENTURY SAMPLER

May the roof above us
never fall in,
and may we friends
gathered below never fall out.

IRISH TOAST

May friendship like wine, improve as time
advances. And may we always have old wine,
old friends, and young cares.

TRADITIONAL

I wish you friends, kind friends who care
for you when you are low, who can teach you
to laugh again.

HELEN THOMSON, B.1943

To your good health, my friend,
may you live for a thousand years,
and I be there to count them.

ROBERT SMITH SURTEES
(1803-1864)

Laugh and be merry together... Glad till the
dancing stops, and the lilt of the music ends.
Laugh till the game is played; and be you
merry my friends.

JOHN MASEFIELD (1878-1967)

Keep on looking for the bright, bright skies;

Keep on hoping that the sun will rise;

Keep on singing when the whole world sighs,

And you'll get there in the morning.

A SONG, AUTHOR UNKNOWN

KEEP A GREEN TREE IN YOUR HEART AND PERHAPS THE SINGING BIRD WILL COME.

CHINESE PROVERB

...find your own way; go with confidence, and expect good things to happen.

LYNNE GERARD

WISHING YOU COURAGE

May fearlessness guard us behind and before!
May fearlessness surround us above and below!
May we be without fear of friend and foe!
May we be without fear of the unknown!
May we be without fear by night and by day!
Let all the world be my friend!

TRANSLATED BY RAIMUNDO PANNIKER,
FROM "THE VEDAS"

Fly free. Fly high and far. Your wings are strong.
There will be times when much will
be asked of you.
I wish you the courage and endurance
and the wisdom you need.
My thoughts are with you always.

PAM BROWN, B.1928

LONG LIFE!

May your age be as old as a mountain
and your happiness as deep as the sea.

AUTHOR UNKNOWN

I am an old man, but in many senses
a very young man. And this is what I want you
to be – young, young all your life,
and to say things to the world that are true.

PABLO CASALS (1876-1973)

I wish you, every birthday, some new love of lovely things, and some new forgetfulness of the teasing things, and some higher pride in the praising things, and some sweeter peace from the hurrying things and some closer fence from the worrying things. And longer stay of time when you are happy and lighter flight of days that are unkind.

JOHN RUSKIN (1819-1900)

May you live all the days of your life.

JONATHAN SWIFT
(1667-1745)

What is a *Helen Exley Giftbook?*

Helen Exley has been creating giftbooks for twenty-six years, and her readers have bought forty-eight million copies of her works, in over thirty languages. Because her books are all bought as gifts, she spares no expense in making sure that each book is as thoughtful and meaningful a gift as it is possible to create: good to give, good to receive. Friendship and kindness, so central to *My Wishes for You,* are very important to Helen, and she has now created several titles on these themes.

Team members help to find thoughtful quotations from literally hundreds of sources, and the books are then personally created. With infinite care, Helen ensures that each illustration matches each quotation, that each spread is individually designed to enhance the feeling of the words, and that the whole book has real depth and meaning.

You have the result in your hands. If you have loved it – tell others! We'd rather put the money into more good books than waste it on advertising when there is no power on earth like the word-of-mouth recommendation of friends.

Helen Exley Giftbooks
16 Chalk Hill, Watford, Herts WD19 4BG, UK.
185 Main Street, Spencer, MA 01562, USA.
www.helenexleygiftbooks.com

Acknowledgements: the publishers are grateful for permission to reproduce copyright material. Whilst every reasonable effort has been made to trace copyright holders, we would be pleased to hear from any not acknowledged. PABLO CASALS: From *Joys and Sorrows* by Albert Kahn, copyright © Albert Kahn 1970. Used by permission of Gillon Aitken Associates Ltd. THICH NHAT HANH: Reprinted from *A Joyful Path* (1994) by Thich Nhat Hanh with permission of Parallax Press, Berkeley, California. IRISH TOASTS pp.7, 16,17 courtesy of Jameson Irish Whiskey. JOHN MASEFIELD: From *Laugh and Be Merry* by John Masefield. Used by permission of The Society of Authors as the Literary Representatives of the Estate of John Masefield. J. DONALD WALTERS: from *"There's Joy in the Heavens"*, published by Crystal Clarity Publishers. Used with permission. PAM BROWN, HELEN EXLEY, CHARLOTTE GRAY, PETER GRAY, STUART & LINDA MACFARLANE, MAYA V. PATEL, HELEN THOMSON: published with permission © Helen Exley 2002.